ORIGINAL KEYS
for SINGERS

PIANO / VOCAL

BROADWAY HITS
FOR MALE SINGERS

T0101615

ISBN 978-1-4803-4128-9

HAL•LEONARD®
CORPORATION
7777 W. BLUEMOUND RD. P.O. BOX 13819 MILWAUKEE, WI 53213

Visit Hal Leonard Online at
www.halleonard.com

ALL I ASK OF YOU

from THE PHANTOM OF THE OPERA

Music by ANDREW LLOYD WEBBER
Lyrics by CHARLES HART
Additional Lyrics by RICHARD STILGOE

BRING HIM HOME
from LES MISERABLES

Music by CLAUDE-MICHEL SCHONBERG
Lyrics by HERBERT KRETZMER and ALAIN BOUBLIL

Music and Lyrics Copyright © 1986 by Alain Boublil Music Ltd. (ASCAP)
Mechanical and Publication Rights for the U.S.A. Administered by Alain Boublil Music Ltd. (ASCAP) c/o Joel Faden & Co., Inc.,
MLM 250 West 57th St., 26th Floor, New York, NY 10107, Tel. (212) 246-7203, Fax (212) 246-7217, mwlock@joelfaden.com

Can You Feel The Love Tonight

Disney Presents THE LION KING: THE BROADWAY MUSICAL

Music by ELTON JOHN
Lyrics by TIM RICE

There's a time __ for ev - 'ry - one

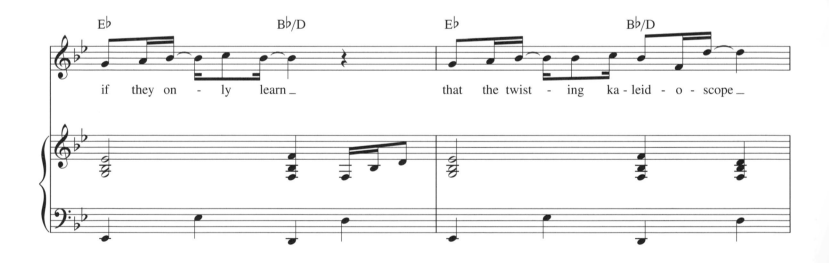

if they on - ly learn __ that the twist - ing ka - leid - o - scope __

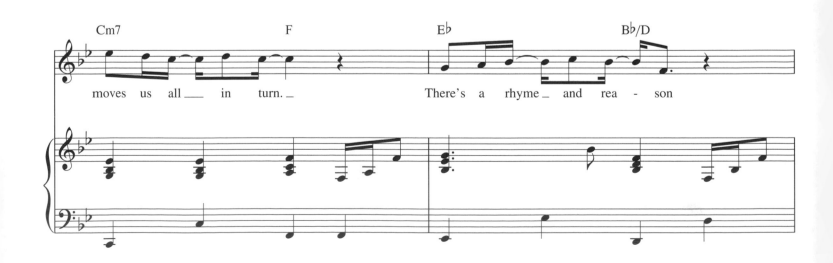

moves us all __ in turn. __ There's a rhyme __ and rea - son

to the wild out-doors, when the heart of this star-crossed voy-ag-er

beats in time with yours.

D.S. al Coda

And

CODA

It's e-nough to make

kings and vag-a-bonds be-lieve the ver-y best.

CIRCLE OF LIFE

Disney Presents THE LION KING: THE BROADWAY MUSICAL

Music by ELTON JOHN
Lyrics by TIM RICE

FALLING SLOWLY
from the Broadway Musical ONCE

Words and Music by GLEN HANSARD
and MARKETA IRGLOVA

Moderately slow

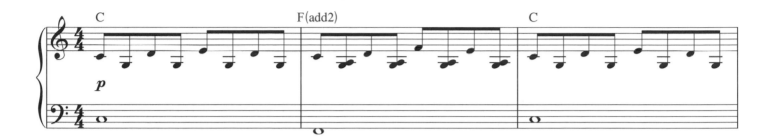

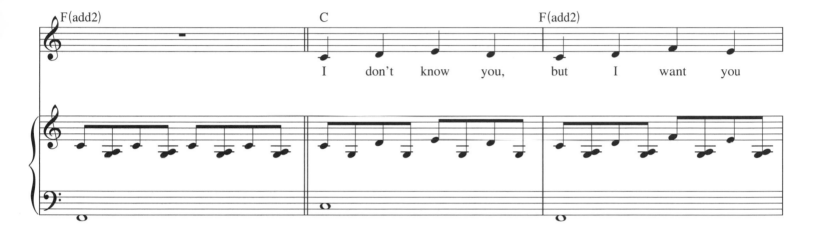

I don't know you, but I want you

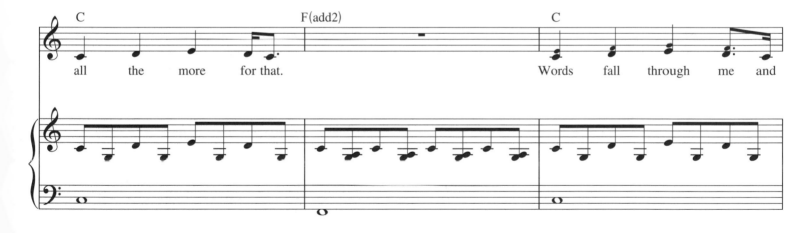

all the more for that. Words fall through me and

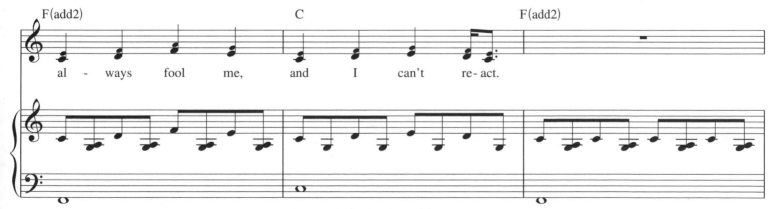

al-ways fool me, and I can't re-act.

Lyrics:
now. _____ Fall - ing slow - ly, eyes that know me and I can't go back. And moods that take me and e - rase me, and I'm paint - ed black. Well, you have suf-fered e - nough and warred with your -

Now you're gone. ___

HEY THERE
from THE PAJAMA GAME

Words and Music by RICHARD ADLER
and JERRY ROSS

IF EVER I WOULD LEAVE YOU

from CAMELOT

Words by ALAN JAY LERNER
Music by FREDERICK LOEWE

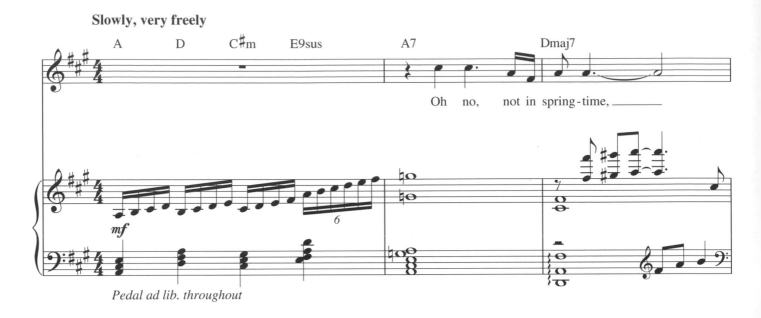

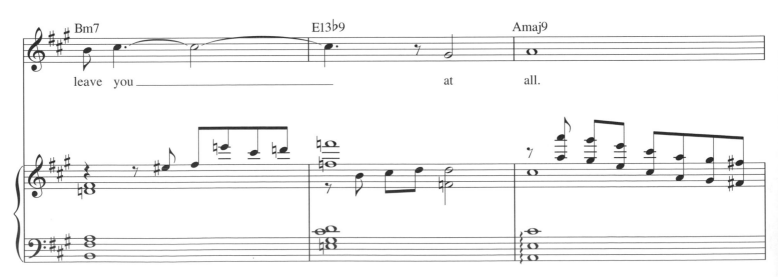

THE IMPOSSIBLE DREAM
(The Quest)
from MAN OF LA MANCHA

Lyric by JOE DARION
Music by MITCH LEIGH

Moderately slow

To dream ___ the im-pos-si-ble dream; to fight ___ the un-beat-a-ble foe; to bear ___ with un-bear-a-ble sor-row; to

LUCK BE A LADY
from GUYS AND DOLLS

By FRANK LOESSER

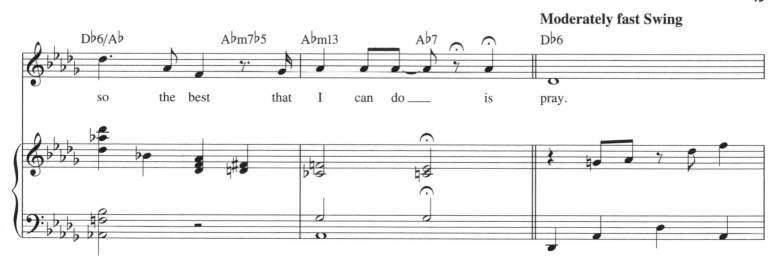

Moderately fast Swing

so the best that I can do ___ is pray.

Luck, be ___ a la - dy ___ to - night.

50

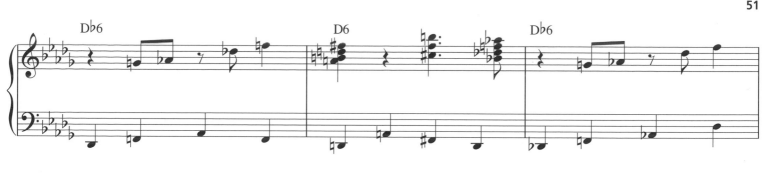

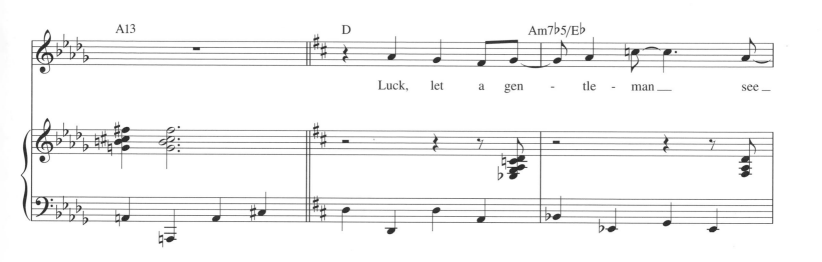

Luck, let a gen - tle - man __ see __

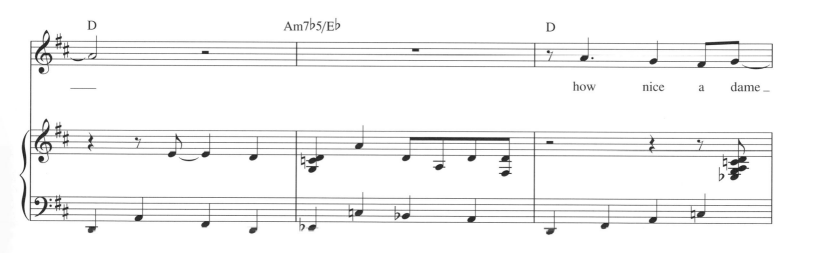

__ how nice a dame __

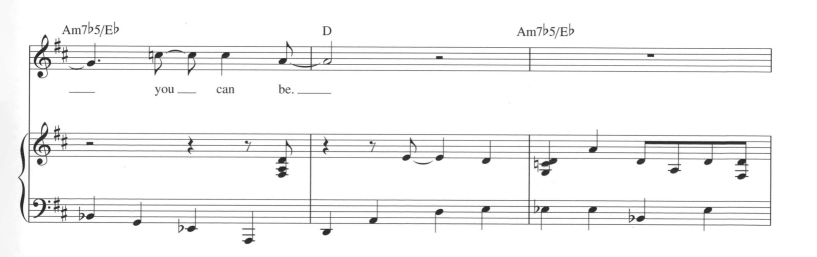

__ you __ can be. ____

I know the way ___ you've treat - ed oth - er guys ___ you've been ___ ___ with.

Luck, be ___ a la - dy ___ with me.

A la - dy does - n't leave ___ her es -

- la you came in with. Luck, be a la-

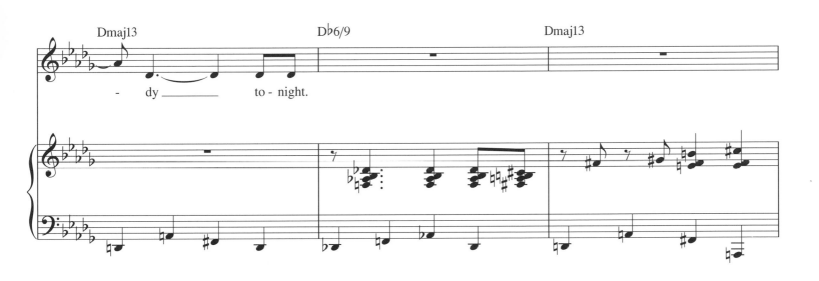

- dy to - night.

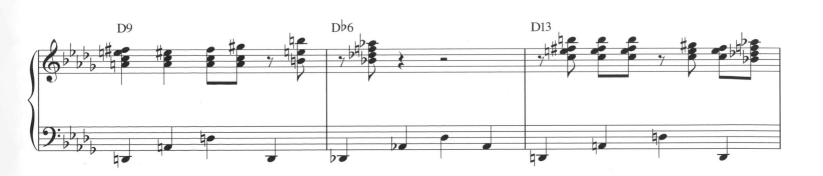

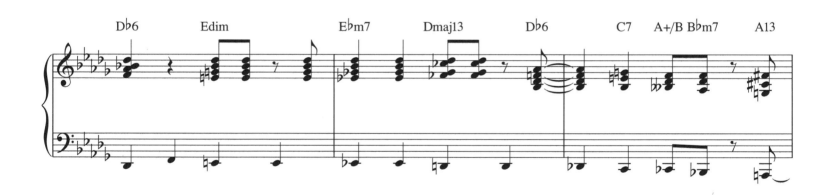

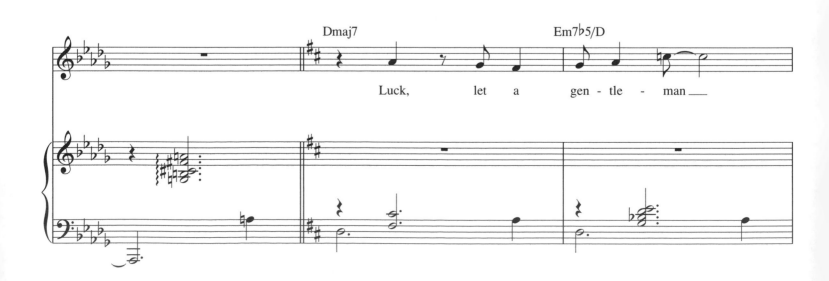

Luck, let a gen - tle - man ___

LULLABY OF BROADWAY

from GOLD DIGGERS OF 1935
from 42ND STREET

Words by AL DUBIN
Music by HARRY WARREN

The rum-ble ___ of the sub-way train, ___ the rat-tle of the

tax - is. ___ The daf-fo-dils who en-ter-tain ___

at An-ge-lo's and Max-i's. When a Broad-way ba-by

says good-night, ___ it's ear-ly in the morn-ing.

Moderately, steadily

Additional lyrics

Female: I'm sorry, show business isn't for me. I'm going back to Allentown.
Male: What was that word you just said? "Allentown?" I'm offering you a
chance to star in the biggest musical Broadway's seen in twenty years,
and you say, "Allentown"?

MAME
from MAME

Music and Lyric by
JERRY HERMAN

THE MUSIC OF THE NIGHT
from THE PHANTOM OF THE OPERA

Music by Andrew LLOYD WEBBER
Lyrics by CHARLES HART
Additional Lyrics by RICHARD STILGOE

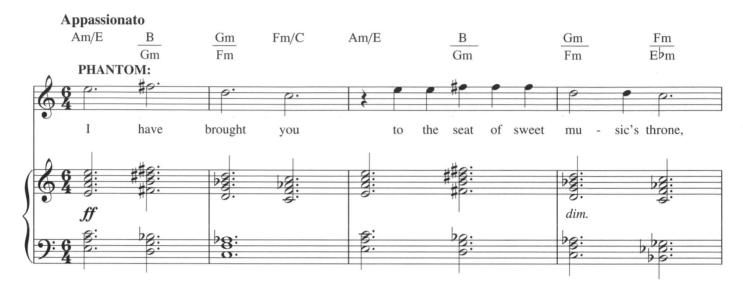

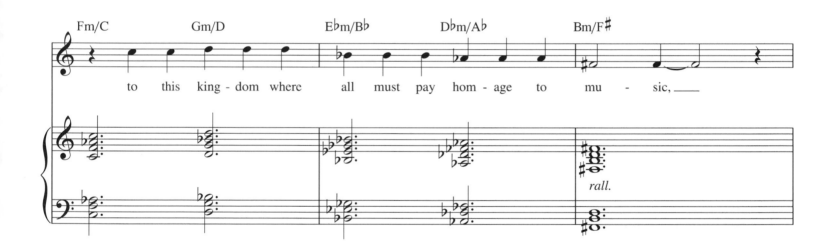

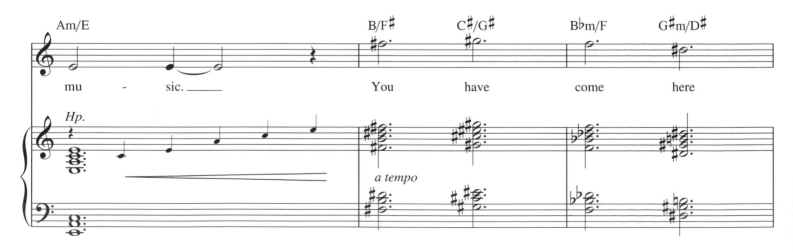

OH, WHAT A BEAUTIFUL MORNIN'
from OKLAHOMA!

Lyrics by OSCAR HAMMERSTEIN II
Music by RICHARD RODGERS

Moderately fast

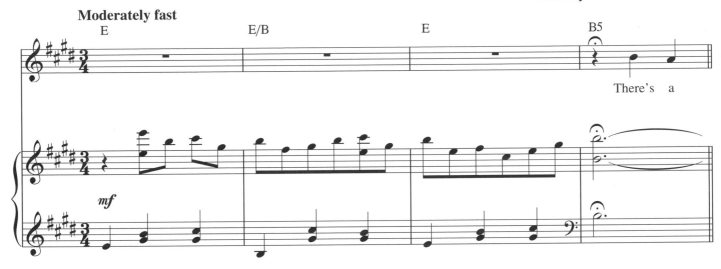

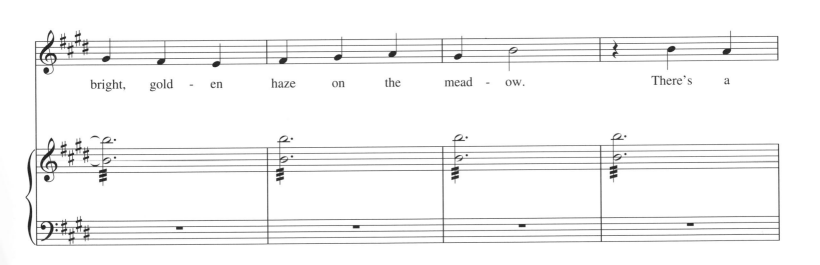

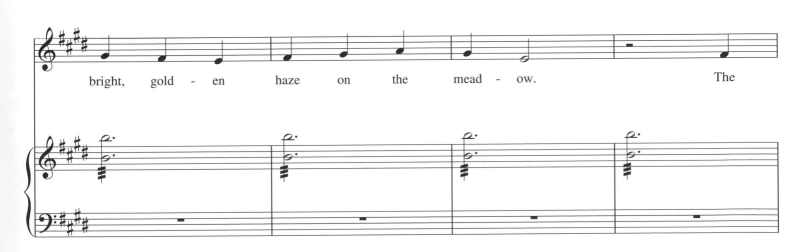

corn is as high as a el - e - phant's eye and it

Moderately

looks like it's climb - ing clear up to the sky.

rit.

Tempo I

Oh, what a beau - ti - ful morn - ing!

Oh, what a beau - ti - ful day!

OH WHAT A CIRCUS

from EVITA

Words by TIM RICE
Music by ANDREW LLOYD WEBBER

ON THE STREET WHERE YOU LIVE

from MY FAIR LADY

Words by ALAN JAY LERNER
Music by FREDERICK LOEWE

Moderately, in 2

PUT ON A HAPPY FACE

from BYE BYE BIRDIE

Lyric by LEE ADAMS
Music by CHARLES STROUSE

SEVENTY SIX TROMBONES

from Meredith Willson's THE MUSIC MAN

By MEREDITH WILLSON

Moderately fast, in 2

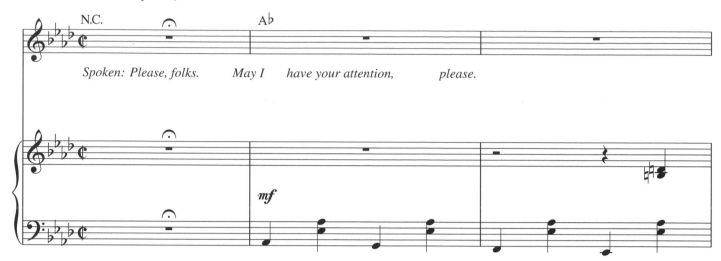

Spoken: Please, folks. May I have your attention, please.

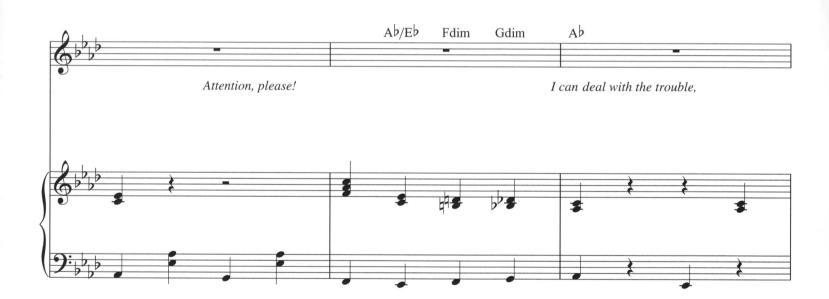

Attention, please! I can deal with the trouble,

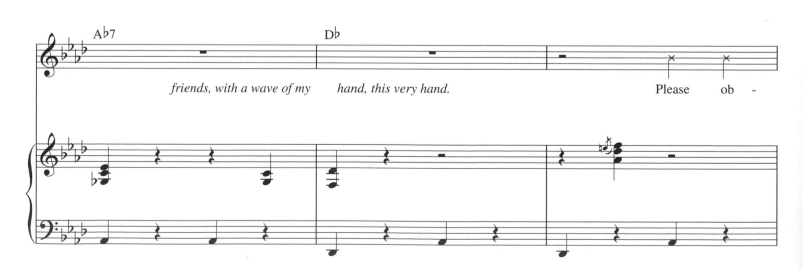

friends, with a wave of my hand, this very hand. Please ob-

thun - der - ing, thun - der - ing loud - er than be -

fore; clar - i - nets of ev - 'ry size, and trum - pet - ers who'd

im - pro - vise a full oc - tave high - er than the score!

Sev - en - ty six trom - bones hit the coun - ter - point

123

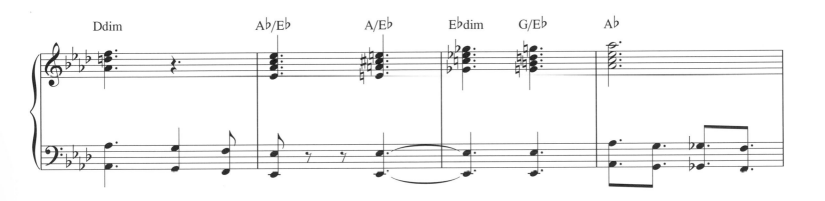

Additional Lyrics

And you'll see the glitter of crashing cymbals,
And you'll hear the thunder of rolling drums,
The shimmer of trumpets! Tah-ta-raah!
And you'll feel something akin to the electrtic thrill I once enjoyed
When Gilmore, Liberati, Pat Conway, the Greate Creatore,
W.C. Handy and John Philip Sousa
All came to town on the very same historic day!

SINGIN' IN THE RAIN

from SINGIN' IN THE RAIN

Lyric by ARTHUR FREED
Music by NACIO HERB BROWN

danc - in' in the rain.

SOME ENCHANTED EVENING

from SOUTH PACIFIC

Lyrics by OSCAR HAMMERSTEIN II
Music by RICHARD RODGERS

SUDDENLY
from LES MISERABLES

Music by CLAUDE-MICHEL SCHONBERG
Lyrics by HERBERT KRETZMER and ALAIN BOUBLIL

Ballad, with rubato

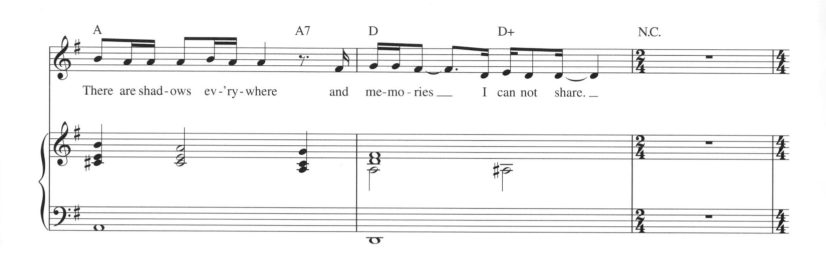

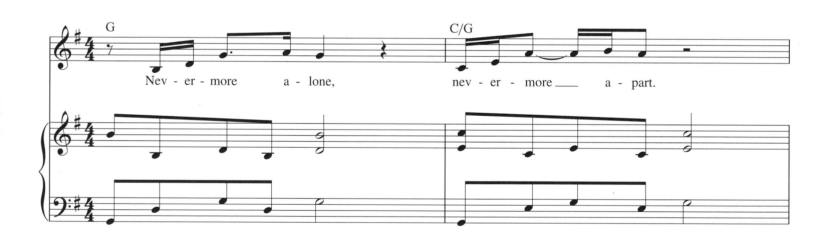

THIS IS THE MOMENT
from JEKYLL & HYDE

Words and Music by LESLIE BRICUSSE
and FRANK WILDHORN

TRY TO REMEMBER

from THE FANTASTICKS

Words by TOM JONES
Music by HARVEY SCHMIDT

YOU'LL BE IN MY HEART

Disney Presents TARZAN The Broadway Musical

Words and Music by
PHIL COLLINS

For one so small, you seem so strong. My arms will hold you, keep you

safe and warm. This bond be-tween us can't be brok - en.

I will be here, don't you cry. 'Cause you'll be in my

heart. Yes, you'll be in my heart from

When des-ti-ny __ calls __ you, __ you must be __ strong. __ I

may not be with you but you've got to hold __ on. ___ They'll __ see in time,

I _____ know. __ We'll show them __ to-geth - er. __ 'Cause

you'll be in __ my __ heart. Be-lieve me, you'll be in ___ my ___